STORYLANDS

Lost Island

READ

The Abandoned Egg

Written by Lisa Thompson

Paintings by Ritva Voutila

INTRODUCTION

Tickles, the pterodactyl, finds a very large, abandoned egg. She wants her friends to help her look after the egg until it hatches. Who could the egg belong to?

SETTING

A clearing on Lost Island

CHARACTERS

Narrator

Tickles

River

Pebble

Leo

Luna

Trio

Rex

Baby dragon
Mother dragon
(not speaking parts)

3

Narrator: While out on her morning flight around the island, Tickles, the pterodactyl, spotted a very large, abandoned, silver egg. She flew down to take a closer look.

Tickles: Oh what a big, beautiful egg you are! I have never seen a silver egg before. In fact you are the largest egg I have ever seen.

Narrator: Tickles felt the egg and could feel something moving inside.

Tickles: I wonder who could have abandoned a big and beautiful egg like you. But you don't have to worry. Now that I have found you, I will build you a big nest. My friends and I will look after you until you hatch.

Narrator: Tickles called to her friends who lived nearby.

Tickles: River and Pebble, come and help.

River: *(panting after a run)* What's up Tickles? Pebble and I came as fast as we could.

Tickles: I want you and Pebble to see the big, beautiful egg I found. I'd like you to help me.

Pebble: It's HUGE. It's the biggest egg I've ever seen! What kind of dinosaur lays silver eggs?

Tickles: I'm not sure. But we're going to look after it. Whatever is inside can hatch when it's ready.

Pebble: *(shocked)* Are you joking?

Tickles: No, I am not. Now stay here with the egg. I'm going off to collect some things to build it a nest.

Narrator: Tickles flew away. Pebble and River didn't know what to do. They had never looked after an egg before. River pushed the enormous egg to see if he could move it. Pebble tried to put her arms around it.

River: *(trying his best to move the egg, but nothing happens)* This thing weighs as much as our friend Trio.

Pebble: I can hardly get my arms around it.

Narrator: Tickles returned with twigs to make a nest.

Tickles: Ah! What a good idea Pebble. You're giving the poor abandoned egg a hug. Yes, keep hugging while I make the nest.

Pebble: *(embarrassed)* I wasn't hugging the egg. I wanted to see if I could get my arms around it.

Tickles: Oh don't be embarrassed Pebble. Egg hugging is a wonderful thing.

River: *(teasing)* Yes Pebble, don't be embarrassed to egg hug. *(giggle)*

Pebble: *(not impressed)* I'm going to find some more things for the nest.

Tickles: Could you get some wood? I think we should make a fire. I don't want the egg to get cold. It's a bit too big to sit on, even with the three of us.

Narrator: Pebble went off to get wood for the fire. As Tickles and River began to make the nest, along came their friend Trio, the triceratops.

Trio: Wow! That has to be the most enormous egg I have ever seen! What kind of dinosaur owns that?

Tickles: Shhhhhh! Must you be so loud! Can't you see the egg is trying to sleep? We don't know what kind of dinosaur. It's been abandoned.

Trio: Maybe it's a bad egg. *(laughing)* Get it — a bad egg! *(still laughing at his own joke)* So who's looking after it now?

Tickles: We are. River and I are making a nest for it. Pebble is off finding firewood. We're going to build a fire to keep it warm.

Trio: I thought you sat on eggs to keep them warm.

River: Not all eggs.

Tickles: And this one is far too big for sitting on. Now Trio, make yourself useful. Use that horn on your head to help us move the egg onto the nest.

11

Narrator: Tickles, Trio, and River all tried as hard as they could to roll the egg onto the nest. The egg would not budge. It was far too heavy.

Trio: It's no use. This egg is far too heavy to move. We are just going to have to build the nest around it.

Narrator: So that's what they did. River had just put the last branch down when Rex, the T-rex, came roaring and stomping through the jungle.

Tickles: Slow down Rex! You are disturbing our egg!

Rex: What egg?

Trio: The enormous one right here in this nest.

Rex: Wow! That egg is massive. (*Rex rubs his tummy and shows his teeth.*) Rex really, really, really loves to eat eggs.

Tickles, River, and Trio stand in front of the egg.

Tickles: Well this one is not for eating Rex!

Rex: You three are no fun. Besides, when the mother of that egg comes back and sees you with her egg, you're going to wish I had eaten it. She is going to want to eat you!

Narrator: Rex stomped and roared his way back into the jungle in search of food.

Tickles: *(to the egg)* Don't listen to him. Rex is always grumpy.

Narrator: Suddenly, the egg started to move and shake.

Tickles: Did you see that? I think it's getting ready to hatch.

Narrator: Pebble returned with wood for the fire. The pixies, Luna and Leo, were with her.

Luna: Well, well, well! *(lets out a whistle)* Would you have a look at the size and color of that egg! *(winks at Leo)*

Leo: I can't believe my eyes. What a find!

Trio: It just moved again!

Tickles: Yes! It's almost ready to hatch. Quickly everyone, we must build the fire NOW!

Leo: *(whispering)* Yes, I am sure this egg will like fire. *(winks at Luna)*

Narrator: Everyone helped get the fire ready. Luna and Leo kept smiling and giggling about what a HOT find the egg was. But when the fire was ready, no matter how hard everyone tried, the fire would not light.

Pebble: and River Let's stack the wood again.

Narrator: No one noticed the egg crack open. Out poked a red, scaly head. Everyone turned when the baby coughed.

Trio: What kind of baby dinosaur is that?

Pixies: *(together)* That is no baby dinosaur!

Tickles: *(excited)* He's sooo cute. Look at his big eyes and his adorable nose.

Narrator: Tickles was just about to pat the baby when it spat out a mouthful of fire.

Tickles: Wow! That's amazing. Let's call it Little Red.

Trio: Let's call it Dangerous. It just spat fire!

Pebble: If it's not a baby dinosaur, then what is it?

19

Luna: This, my friends, is a baby dragon.

Trio and: River *(scared and shocked)* A WHAT!

Narrator: Suddenly, everything went dark. They looked up and saw the mother dragon flying overhead.

Trio: This is the end for us. Look out!

Narrator: Little Red let out another spurt of fire and ran to join his mother. Then they both flew off.

Tickles: *(waving)* Bye, bye Little Red. Come back and visit. You're always welcome.

Trio: Are you kidding? That thing could wipe us all out with one breath. That's one dangerous animal.

Tickles: Oh I don't know. He had a real spark about him don't you think?

MAKE SOME SIMPLE PROPS

There is a large silver egg. You need twigs to make a nest and more wood to build a fire.

You will need:

- ✓ A large cardboard box or sheets of cardboard.
- ✓ Sticky tape and glue
- ✓ Silver paint
- ✓ Twigs
- ✓ Pieces of wood
- ✓ Red crepe paper

Make an egg

1. Cut out a very large egg shape from cardboard.
2. Paint the egg silver.
3. Glue the egg shape to a box. (Baby dragon jumps out of the box.)

Dress up as a dragon

1. Wear red tights and a long-sleeved shirt.
2. Make a red tail to attach at back.
3. Make dragon wings out of crepe paper. Stick them to your arms.
4. Wear a dragon mask.

Who wanted to eat the egg?

Why did Tickles want to build a fire?

How would you look after an abandoned egg?

What could Trio use to try to move the egg?

Why do you think Tickles was sad when the dragons flew off?